A Smart Kid's Guide to
Avoiding Online Predators

David J. Jakubiak

PowerKiDS
press
New York

Published in 2010 by The Rosen Publishing Group, Inc.
29 East 21st Street, New York, NY 10010

First Edition

Editor: Amelie von Zumbusch
Book Design: Julio Gil
Photo Researcher: Jessica Gerweck

Photo Credits: Cover © www.iStockphoto.com/Nina Shannon; p. 5 photos_alyson/Getty Images; p. 6 © George Shelley/age fotostock; p. 9 © Philippe Lissac/Godong/Corbis; p. 10 © www.iStockphoto.com/Rob Bouwman; p. 13 Walter Hodges/Getty Images; p. 14 Zia Soleil/Getty Images; p. 17 Joe Raedle/Getty Images; p. 18 Shutterstock.com; p. 21 Bruce Laurance/Getty Images.

Library of Congress Cataloging-in-Publication Data

Jakubiak, David J.
  A smart kid's guide to avoiding online predators / David J. Jakubiak. — 1st ed.
    p. cm. — (Kids online)
  Includes index.
  ISBN 978-1-4042-8117-2 (library binding : alk. paper) — ISBN 978-1-4358-3354-8 (pbk.) — ISBN 978-1-4358-3355-5 (6-pack)
  1. Internet and children—Juvenile literature. 2. Internet—Safety measures. 3. Safety education—Juvenile literature. 4. Children and strangers—Juvenile literature. I. Title.
  HQ784.I58J36 2010
  004.67'80289—dc22
                                    2009004343

Manufactured in the United States of America

Contents

Danger on the Web

The Internet is like a giant park. You can play games there. You can discover many interesting things. You can even meet up with friends. With so much to do, though, you need to remember to be safe.

When you go to a park, you watch out for strangers. On the Internet, you need to watch out for online predators. These bad people use the Internet to try to meet children. They try to become friends with kids and ask them to do things that kids should not do. Knowing how to deal with online predators will help you stay safe when you are having fun online.

You might feel shocked or upset if an online predator reaches out to you. These people send messages or pictures that kids should not have to read or see.

Always remember that you cannot
tell if people are telling the truth online. Do not believe
everything that a person tells you online.

Who Is Out There?

In a public place, such as a park, you can learn certain things about a stranger. You can look at a person and hear his or her voice. However, this is not possible online. People can invent **identities** online. They can pick new names. They can lie about their ages. People can make up where they live. They can even use another person's picture as their own picture.

No matter how many times you chat with a person online, remember that you do not know who that person really is. Online predators often pretend to be people they are not. They may even pretend to be kids.

How Problems Start

Online predators try to meet kids on sites where young people hang out, such as **chat rooms**. After predators read chats, they may send **private** messages to kids. Online predators also leave notes on Web sites and send messages by e-mail. Predators sometimes reach out to kids while they are playing online games that let players talk to each other.

If a predator **contacts** you, the first messages may sound like they are from a friend. They may ask, "What's up?" Then, the predator may ask for your real name or age. However, you should never answer questions from a stranger. You do not even need to write back.

If you think that a message you received may have come from a predator, do not read the whole thing. Move on to another e-mail message or Web site as soon as you feel unsafe.

Do not let the idea of online predators keep you from using the Internet. You should be careful online, but you do not need to be afraid of using the World Wide Web.

Keeping Your Cool

There are times when a predator may reach out to you more than once. This is the way predators try to become **familiar** with you and earn your trust. Over time, predators may send messages in which they try to get more and more **information** from you.

Predators often ask if they can send pictures to you. They may also want you to send pictures of yourself to them. They may offer to send you presents. These bad people may even ask you to do things that make you feel uncomfortable. Getting messages from a predator can be very scary and upsetting. However, there are several ways you can take control.

Fighting Back

If a predator is sending you messages, it is not your fault. It does not matter if the message comes in a chat room, by e-mail, or while you are playing a game. You are not alone. Do not feel **embarrassed** or trapped. Instead, put a stop to the messages.

The best thing to do if a predator sends you messages is to tell an adult. Your parents, guardians, or teachers are all good adults to tell. Go online with the adults and show them the messages that you received. Tell the adults everything that happened. Together, make a plan to keep the predator from bothering you.

Even if you are embarrassed by the messages you have received, it is very important to tell a trusted adult if an online predator has contacted you.

If you are worried about telling the police about an online predator, first go over what happened with an adult with whom you are close. This may make talking to the police easier.

Getting Help

Online predators are criminals. The things they do are against the law. If anyone asks you to do something that does not seem right or sends you **inappropriate** pictures or movies, tell an adult who can contact the police. You may feel uncomfortable and scared, and that is okay. Remember that the predator is the person who did something wrong, not you. The police know how to deal with predators and can help you.

If you have messages, pictures, or movies that a predator has sent you, tell the police about all of them. Do not print any of these things. Instead, ask the police what you should do with them.

Going After a Predator

The police will ask you questions when you report an online predator. They may also ask to check your computer. This will let them take a good look at any messages that you have received from a predator.

There are many ways police officers can go after online predators. They can use the messages that kids report. They can also set up sting operations in which police officers go into chat rooms and pretend to be kids. The officers who are pretending to be kids may even set up real-life meetings with predators. When the predators show up, the police officers **arrest** them.

When police officers arrest online predators,
they often take the predators' computers away. This lets the
officers gather evidence against the predators.

The Internet offers many ways to learn, have fun, and share your thoughts. Be careful not to share too much about yourself, though.

18

Keeping Yourself Safe

There are ways to lower your chances of ever hearing from an online predator. You likely already know that telling anyone online your real name, age, or where you live is a bad idea. Keeping this information out of **online profiles** is important, too. Also keep facts such as your school name, team names, phone number, and e-mail address to yourself. These can all be used to reach you.

Stay away from sites with chat rooms that are not watched over by adults. Do not post pictures of yourself online. Share your e-mail address or instant-messaging contact only with your family and very best friends.

Keep It Online

Before talking to people online, talk with your parents or guardian. Come up with a list of rules about what you are allowed to do online. Visit some sites together and pick which ones are right for you. One rule every kid should have is that you will never agree to meet a person whom you met online in person.

When you are online, it may not seem like you are in public. However, a trip online is like a trip to a park. You must be careful of strangers. This does not mean you always have to be scared. Just make sure to be safe when you are having fun online.

You can always ask a trusted adult to help you find Web sites that are safe to visit. This will help you avoid online predators.

Safety Tips

- Do not meet people whom you met online in person.

- Pick a **screen name** that hides your real identity.

- Do not share your **passwords** with your friends or with people you meet online.

- Never give out your phone number or call a number that was given to you by someone you met online.

- Open messages only from people you know.

- If something in a message does not seem right, tell an adult.

- Always remember that you can never really know to whom you are talking when you are online.

- Talk to a trusted adult before visiting sites that let you talk to strangers.

Glossary

arrest (uh-REST) To catch people who are thought to have committed crimes.

chat rooms (CHAT ROOMZ) Online places where people can type messages to each other.

contacts (KON-takts) Talks or meets with a person.

embarrassed (em-BAR-usd) Full of shame or uneasiness.

familiar (fuh-MIL-yer) Well known, or common.

identities (eye-DEN-tuh-teez) Who people are.

inappropriate (in-nuh-PROH-pree-ut) Not suitable or right.

information (in-fer-MAY-shun) Knowledge or facts.

online profiles (AWN-lyn PROH-fy-elz) Information about themselves that people enter to be stored on Web sites.

passwords (PAS-wurdz) Secret combinations of letters or numbers that let people enter something.

private (PRY-vit) Alone or cannot be seen by others.

screen name (SKREEN NAYM) A name someone uses online.

Index

Web Sites

Due to the changing nature of Internet links, PowerKids Press has developed an online list of Web sites related to the subject of this book. This site is updated regularly. Please use this link to access the list: www.powerkidslinks.com/onlin/predator/

ML   12/09